Quilt National 2011

Quilt National 2011

The Best of Contemporary Quilts

Co-produced by
Lark Crafts & The Dairy Barn Arts Center

LARK CRAFTS

An Imprint of Sterling Publishing Co., Inc.
New York

WWW.LARKCRAFTS.COM

Quilt National Director
Kathleen M. Dawson

Senior Editor
Valerie Van Arsdale Shrader

Copy Editor
Suzanne J.E. Tourtillott

Art Director
Megan Kirby

Art Assistant
Meagan Shirlen

Photographers
Gary J. Kirksey
Larry Hamel-Lambert
Sam Girton

Cover Designer
Megan Kirby

Cover
Judy Kirpich, page 88

Half-title page, top to bottom
Mary E. Stoudt, page 108
Katie Pasquini Masopust, page 100

Title page, top to bottom
Bette Uscott-Woolsey, page 96
Judy Rush, page 75
Bonnie M. Bucknam, page 43

Contents page, top to bottom
Sue Cavanaugh, page 50
Katherine K. Allen, page 28
Daphne Taylor, page 61

Page 17, top to bottom
Lisa Call, page 95
Jean M. Evans, page 76
Judy Kirpich, page 88

Library of Congress Cataloging-in-Publication Data
Quilt National (2011 : Athens, Ohio)
  Quilt National 2011 : The Best of Contemporary Quilts / Co-produced by
Lark Crafts & The Dairy Barn Arts Center. -- First Edition.
      pages cm
  Includes index.
  ISBN 978-1-60059-799-2
  1. Art quilts--United States--History--21st century--Exhibitions. 2. Art quilts--History--
21st century--Exhibitions. I. Lark Crafts (Firm) II. Dairy Barn Arts Center. III. Title.
  NK9112.Q5 2011
  746.460973'07477197--dc22

                        2010047692

10 9 8 7 6 5 4 3 2 1

First Edition

Published by Lark Crafts
An Imprint of Sterling Publishing Co., Inc.
387 Park Avenue South, New York, NY 10016

Text © 2011, Lark Crafts, an Imprint of Sterling Publishing Co., Inc.
Photography © 2011, Lark Crafts, an Imprint of Sterling Publishing Co., Inc.,
unless otherwise specified

Distributed in Canada by Sterling Publishing,
c/o Canadian Manda Group, 165 Dufferin Street
Toronto, Ontario, Canada M6K 3H6

Distributed in the United Kingdom by GMC Distribution Services,
Castle Place, 166 High Street, Lewes, East Sussex, England BN7 1XU

Distributed in Australia by Capricorn Link (Australia) Pty Ltd.,
P.O. Box 704, Windsor, NSW 2756 Australia

If you have questions or comments about this book, please contact:
Lark Crafts
67 Broadway
Asheville, NC 28801
828-253-0467

Manufactured in China

ISBN 13: 978-1-60059-799-2

For information about custom editions, special sales, premium and corporate
purchases, please contact Sterling Special Sales Department at 800-805-5489 or
specialsales@sterlingpub.com.

For information about desk and examination copies available to college
and university professors, requests must be submitted to academic@larkbooks.com.
Our complete policy can be found at www.larkcrafts.com.

Contents

Foreword

In 1979 the Quilt National exhibition was described as one that embraced the departure from the traditional past and an exhibition that continues to foster artistic innovation and diversity in the contemporary quilt world. This year marks the 17th biennial installment of the international, juried exhibition of Quilt National. This year more than 1,000 works were submitted by artists from 46 states and 22 foreign countries for the opportunity to be chosen for Quilt National 2011. These artists represent the foundation of what Quilt National is and the future of the art quilt medium.

On behalf of the entire staff and Board of Trustees, I would like to extend our gratitude to the businesses, organizations, and individuals whose generosity in time and financial support make it possible for the Dairy Barn Arts Center to produce this exhibition, which showcases the work of some of the most talented professional and emerging artists working in the medium. An exhibition like this is not possible without the contributions and insight of many individuals. The corps of volunteers, jurors, and artists guided by Kathleen Dawson, Quilt National Director, work tirelessly to produce this exhibition. The Dairy Barn is grateful for the insight and careful consideration of Eleanor McCain, Pauline Verbeek-Cowart, and Nelda Warkentin, the jurors of this exhibit, who selected thought-provoking works that showcase current trends in the world of contemporary quilt art created by artists from around the world. Their collective talents and insight created an engaging exhibition certain to elicit positive responses and encourage stimulating interactions among viewers and participants.

Works in fiber were not meant to be experienced in two dimensions. Works in fiber are intended to be experienced firsthand, to allow the viewer to discover the nuances in surface texture and variations in color, and to appreciate the details articulated in stitches. This catalog is a printed record that documents the exhibition in its entirety and illustrates the diverse methods and processes of artists working in the medium today. Over the past three decades, Quilt National has included work from more than 1,400 artists, many of whom were pioneers in the contemporary art quilt movement and many who continue to reveal new directions in the medium.

Andrea Lewis
Executive Director
Dairy Barn Arts Center

Major support for this exhibition is provided by:

The Robert and Ardis James Foundation

Quilts Japan Magazine / Nihon Vogue Company, Limited

Friends of Fiber Art International

Fairfield Processing

Athens County Convention and Visitor's Bureau

With additional support from the following businesses and organizations:

Aaron's

Hampton Inn

Honeyfork Fabrics

Nelsonville Quilt Company

Ohio University Inn and Conference Center

Ohio Quilts!!

Porter Financial Services

The Regional Nonprofit Alliance at the Voinovich School

Studio Art Quilt Associates, Incorporated

And the following generous individuals:

Betty Goodwin

Bobby and Katie Masopust

The McCarthy Family

Special thanks to:

Ron Dawson

Marvin Fletcher

Dee Fogt

Liz Gillam

Nancy Nottke

David Stobbart

Introduction

In 2009 Quilt National celebrated its 30th year, and we congratulated ourselves for the continuation and growth of what has become a focal exhibition for the art quilt medium. Now that we have passed that milestone, it is time to reach out to a new generation (or two) of artists who have embraced a medium that has far more opportunities in this country and around the world than were even to be imagined in 1979. In addition to galleries and museums that have embraced it as a most popular exhibition format, there are forums around the world in which experienced artists share new techniques with one another and with emerging artists. With the advent of the Internet, communication across the globe is commonplace and works can be seen and shared by artists working on many different continents. Exhibition venues in Australia, Japan, Europe, and the breadth of the United States are suddenly available to artists from all over the world.

So, the Quilt National mission for the next biennium is to celebrate the past success of having established our mission to bring art quilts to the world and to broaden that mission by encouraging younger artists to brave the competition and offer their new work and their fresh perspectives to the jurying process. Whenever I travel and have the opportunity to speak to groups of art quilters, the questions inevitably turn to the Quilt National entries and the mystery that seems to surround the process through which each biennial exhibition is chosen. The quilters seem to believe that there is some sort of system that makes it very difficult to break the barrier between Quilt National entrant and Quilt National exhibitor. The truth of the matter is that we have an excellent process in place that has been refined through years of practice. Let me share that with you now.

The Dairy Barn staff goes to great lengths to make the jury process as fair as we possibly can make it. The process begins with the selection of jurors. They are chosen 12 to 18 months in advance of each competition. As a general rule, two of the jurors are

Kate Themel, *Dandelion* (detail)

artists who are currently working in the field and have achieved a level of name recognition. The third juror is chosen for the purpose of bringing a different perspective to the proceedings. We have had museum and gallery curators, artists from other media, authors, and representatives in academia. These individuals are familiar with and supportive of the art quilt medium, but provide a viewpoint of artwork that augments that of the two artists. The particular group chemistry that results from the collaboration of the three jurors is critical to the makeup of the exhibition in any given year. Initially, the show's strength is determined by the overall quality of the entries and by the collective vision of the jurors as they sift through the 1,000–1,400 images. These two factors are always variable from biennium to biennium; the entrant pool is fluid and the jurors are always different. What this means for the entrant is that there are no "objective criteria" that are constant from jury to jury. The individual artist cannot target their work in a particular direction,

Tanya A. Brown, *Farmer Brown* (detail)

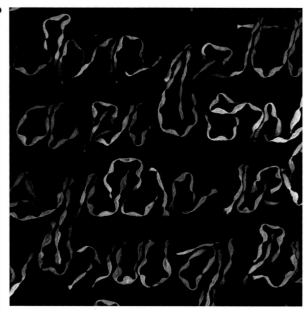

Naomi S. Adams, *Greek* (detail)

a particular format, or a particular subject because the next jury panel will be looking at things in an entirely different way! What is consistent from jury to jury is the charge to select works "that demonstrate the breadth and diversity of contemporary expressions."

Strong, visually compelling compositions initially rise to the top of the jurors' selections. Poor photography is an almost automatic rejection in the early rounds—the jurors have 10 seconds to view the image and make an initial judgment. That does not allow them time to wonder about what they are seeing. Jurors are not permitted to discuss works for the first three rounds, so they make judgments relying on their own expertise and the quality of the images presented to them. Jurors score the works on a scale of 1 to 4. The scores are added together and the composite score determines whether a piece advances to the next round. Only works that are scored very low (meaning 1) by at least two jurors do not advance to the second round.

The second round is scored in the same manner. The jurors have now seen all of the entries, have had time to process an initial reaction, and now can consider both further aspects of the work itself and its relation to the entire pool of submissions. The difference between the scoring of the two rounds is that the minimum score to advance to the next round is now slightly higher. At least one juror has to be strongly in favor of the work (scoring a 3 or 4) to push it to the next round and the other two jurors have to at least be willing to consider it further.

At this point in the jurying process, we are about halfway to our goal of 85 pieces. Approximately half of the works have been eliminated, we have been sitting in a darkened room looking at quilts for eight to ten hours, and the jurors have what amounts to total sensory overload. So, we take pity on them and do a little of what we have become famous for in Athens, Ohio—we wine and dine them and send them to bed to dream about how they are going to make the final selections!

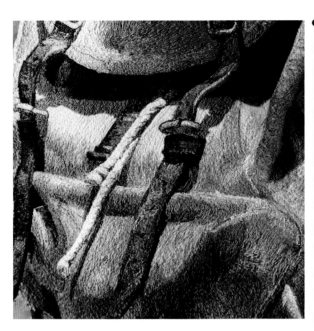

Jayne Bentley Gaskins, *Solitude* (detail)

At the beginning of the second day of judging, the jurors are usually tired of their own counsel and eager to hear how their fellow jurors are processing what they have seen. They are also very anxious to be able to talk and ask questions about materials and techniques! This is the entrants' greatest opportunity to give the jurors additional information about each individual work by taking the time to put as much information as will fit on the entry form. We usually take some time to consult with the jurors and find out what kinds of discussions and processes will help them winnow the numbers further. Some jury panels have chosen to set up a round in which they each vote yes or no on a work in order to advance it to the next round. Some panels have set up a yes-no-maybe round and then see where the numbers stand at the end of that round. As each group of jurors moves through the process, they come to grips with the enormity of the task before them, the limited time frame in which they have to work, and their desire to produce an exhibition that will showcase a broad representation of the art quilt medium to the world audience.

Now we are back to the underlying foundation that sustains this enduring exhibition—the artists and their entries. New artists—whether they are new to the medium, new to the national/international stage, or just starting to exhibit their work—need to be encouraged to use Quilt National as a jumping-off point for their venture into the arena of art exhibitions. We hope that you will find inspiration in the 2011 edition of Quilt National. This new show, which is showcased on the following pages, is representative of a long list of contemporary surface design techniques and a wide variety of traditional quilting techniques. Each piece is a unique presentation of visual art and contemporary expression. Every Quilt National is made up of 85 representative artists. While many artists are repeat exhibitors, the typical makeup of the artist pool is 48% first-time exhibitors. Of that 48%, in 2011, 15% (13 individuals) were chosen on their very first attempt to enter.

My message to all aspiring art quilters is very simple. We need your participation. The continued growth of the art quilt medium needs you to keep working and growing as serious artists. The continued existence of Quilt National and other large art quilt venues is dependent on your participation. The growth of the medium requires an ever-expanding base of artists to feed the demand of the public to see and experience new art quilts. We have come a long way and have grown over the past 30 years, but we are not finished yet!

Kathleen M. Dawson
Quilt National Director
November 2010

Jurors' Statements

Nelda Warkentin

Rewarding describes my experience as a juror. The jury process, which took place at The Dairy Barn Arts Center last September, spanned two days. Evaluating over 1,000 quilts by artists from around the world and seeing the range of styles and techniques was incredible. The high level of imagination, skill, and creativity of the artists was exhilarating. All who entered are to be commended. The time, energy, and expense of submitting are an indication of your commitment to your art. For those who believe their work should have been juried in, your quilt may have been in the final round. To be in the top 15–20% is a significant accomplishment. Keep applying. Your work may be selected next time.

The jurying process offers insights into what makes certain quilts rise to the top. Composition and intentional decision-making by the artist are extremely important. When these two factors are evident, the end result is, more often than not, masterful. Truly exciting were those works where one could honestly say, "I wouldn't change a thing." The quilts in Quilt National 2011 were selected because they met this standard; at least, the digital images we saw lead us to this conclusion. Seeing the quilts in person and deciding whether our initial judgment was correct will be interesting.

I'd like to comment on some of the quilts that received an award:

Judy Kirpich's *Circles #4* (Cathy Rasmussen Emerging Artist Memorial Award) uses color, shape, and texture to float the commanding circles and piercing red lines above quieter, nearly solid, color shapes. Weaving the red lines through the silver and blue circles was a good decision, as it gives the quilt added interest. *Circles #4* is a compelling composition.

In *Con Brio — With Spirit*, by Katie Pasquini Masopust (Quilts Japan Prize), it's exciting to me the way the image moves laterally and at the same time takes the viewer to a place *behind* the surface. The square frames contrast sharply with the vibrant,

Nelda Warkentin

Meadow Pine 2
2009

Silk, cotton, canvas, linen, paint; painted, collaged, machine pieced, machine quilted

70" H x 50" W

The Great White Pine is magnificent because it expresses both strength and beauty.

curved shapes. The use of violet and its complementary hue, yellow, bring intensity to the spirited and energetic image. All are excellent choices.

Striking color in *Color Box #13*, by Shoko Hatano (Persistence Pays Award), captures one's attention. The "safe" machine-quilted background is in stark contrast with the bold markings. Paring a darker palette with brilliant color increases this work's jarring effect. The large, hard-edged, repetitive markings on the surface also oppose the small, curvy, repetitive stitching in the background. Why are there horizontal lines across the background? Why put rectangular shapes in the lower half? I wonder, but I can't imagine doing it any other way. This quilt challenges.

The composition of *Crater*, by Bonnie M. Bucknam (Best of Show), is exciting and well executed. The imaginary lines created by the palette and shapes create a point just to the right of center. Dense quilting supports the landscape and draws my eye up into and around the image. How well the light color in the lower left and dark color on top work! I would have thought the weighted color on the top would be a mistake but in this work the light color pushes the eye up towards the middle. Using irregular edges to reinforce the curved lines within the image is a masterful touch.

Katherine K. Allen's *Glass Garden* (*Diptych*) (McCarthy Memorial Award), has great composition, balance, an interesting use of plant imagery, and perfect scale. The unique horizontal shape encourages me to study the image by looking left and right. Use of a silhouette style against the light background emphasizes the plant contours. The refined palette suggests elegance. This is another quilt where I think to myself, "I wouldn't change a thing."

Greek, by Naomi S. Adams (Most Innovative Use of the Medium), poses some questions: What is this quilt saying? Is it saying anything? The well-placed, light-colored "letters" throughout the work keep my eye moving. Adams has used a unique technique to create a fascinating quilt—a great example of artistic intent that needed to be done in fiber.

Only with fiber and thread can one achieve the look seen in *Ori-Kume 20*, by Sue Cavanaugh (Lynn Goodwin Borgman Award for Surface Design). The tension between the left and right shapes is created largely by the artist's masterful use of texture and a limited palette of dark markings on light fabric. Different but somehow similar shapes on the left and right cause me to wonder what I'm viewing. The texture, markings, and images give this work a strong presence.

Quilt Drawing #13 – for Maureen, by Daphne Taylor, is my choice for a Juror's Award of Merit. This whole cloth quilt is exquisite and executed perfectly. Letting the edges of the inner circle slip gives a soft energy to this quiet work. The straight lines within the large circle contrast with the wisps of line elsewhere. Tiny colorful squares add just the right touch—a bit of interest. The squares also anchor the circles by suggesting imaginary lines that bisect the circles. Every aspect of this quilt has been given careful consideration by the artist.

Balance, movement, and perfect composition make *Structures #113*, by Lisa Call (Award of Excellence), a strong work. Even though the quilt has a limited palette, there is a lot going on that makes the work interesting—lines in different directions created by stitching; slices of fabric, a hint of squares, and other shapes that seem to be floating; and quilting stitches that captivate.

In closing, Quilt National and The Dairy Barn Arts Center are to be commended for conducting a jurying process that focuses on the work and does not favor one artist over another. I can't envision a fairer process. We viewed each work a minimum of three times. On the first day, each juror scored the entries independently. Talking and questions were not allowed. The scoring reduced the number of entries under consideration to less than 200. On the second day, unless there was unanimous consent, we discussed the remaining quilts in depth—focusing on composition, design considerations, and artistic intent. The names of the artists were kept from us until the very end. On the second day, we could ask, "Is this a work by so-and-so?" The reply was only yes or no. Those assisting with the process never volunteered an artist's name. The question, asked only a few times (as we wanted to remain impartial), was intended to reduce the likelihood of derivative work.

After the jury process was completed, the names of the artists were read while we reviewed the images selected. Discovering that we had juried in quilts by many new entrants and artists from around the world was exciting. Thrilling, too, was the announcement that several of the works selected were by established artists working in a new style. In several instances, their names, which we learned after the fact, came as a complete surprise. Learning that we had affirmed their risk-taking was satisfying.

As I write, I wonder what my reaction will be when I view the actual quilts. Which ones will the viewers favor?

To The Dairy Barn Arts Center staff, board members, and volunteers who facilitated the jury process, fed us, gave us rides, and watched over us as Athens experienced a tornado and power outage—a heartfelt thank you. Thank you, too, for the opportunity to participate in a truly rewarding experience.

Thank you to my fellow jurors, Eleanor McCain and Pauline Verbeek-Cowart, for respecting my opinions, for your thoughtful questions and insightful comments.

Thank you to all of the artists who entered. Seeing the images of your work was truly an honor.

Eleanor McCain

What about these works of art demands that they be formed from cloth and thread? Is there a message and meaning that can only be revealed through this medium? What in the quilt form is important to the art? As a fiber art professor once asked, "If it's not about the fiber, why work in that medium?"

Quilts have always been art. Author and professor of art history Patricia Mainardi suggests that quilts were a crucial source of inspiration for modern art, rejecting the view that it was modern art that laid the foundation for seeing quilts as art.[1] Quilts as art did not begin with Rauschenberg, the Bicentennial, or Holstein and the Whitney show. Susan E. Bernick, in "A Quilt Is an Art Object When It Stands Up like a Man," argues that perhaps these were culminating events that allowed or inspired contemporary art quilts to be recognized as art, but that contemporary quilt artists are merely continuing a tradition of art making.[2]

Mainardi has called the quilt "The Great American Art." A quilt can be a physical object, like a bed cover or family heirloom, or a representation of something else. The quilt is laden, even burdened, with symbolism. This single art form can be a metaphor for family, ritual, memory, community, home, and beauty. The idea of "quilt" conveys references to the domestic: women's work, clothing, bedding, protection, comfort, as well as those associated with the bed: sleep, sex, birth, and death. It encompasses significant life events. Because of the familiar symbolism, fiber may be used with irony to emphasize other content. Authors Penny McMorris and Patricia Malarcher have written on feminism and quilting, and the irony of men appropriating, exhibiting, and writing about the meaning of traditional quilts.[3]

Historical references and cultural stereotypes should be considered. Elaine Showalter, literary critic and feminist, suggests, "The patchwork quilt [has come] to replace the melting-pot as the central metaphor of American cultural identity. In a very unusual pattern, it transcended the stigma of its sources in

Eleanor McCain

9 Patch Color Study 7
2010

Cotton, dye, cotton batting, cotton thread; improvisationally
cut, machine pieced, machine quilted

110" H x 109" W

Creativity through the crafting of objects with functional
reference has a place in social pattern. Craft objects reflect
the common experiences of many. Quilting is grounded in
American history, family, community, and common experience. Art quilts are a living document of cultural history
expressing artistic, emotional, and spiritual values, particularly
those of women. I use quilts to transpose function and
symbol, art and craft, and to express ideals about creativity
and community.

women's culture and has been remade as a universal
sign of American identity."[4] Admiration of frugal recy-
cling, creating beauty from scraps of cloth, and the
importance of community work are American icons.
Many feel connected to ancestors who made "works
of the hand," treasured over generations. Traditional
quilts hold the seeds of political comment and dis-
sent. There have been temperance quilts to promote
prohibition, "green" quilts to raise ecological aware-
ness, and quilts used to support specific political
candidates, most recently Barack Obama. Perhaps one
of the largest art pieces ever created is the NAMES
Project Foundation quilt, also known as the AIDS
Memorial Quilt. Quilts have been put to many political
uses, raising consciousness or money.

There are visual characteristics of fiber that awe,
unmatched in other media. Light reflection, the tactile quality of fabric, texture, and the stitched line
are critical elements in works relating to the idea of
"quilt." Considering the best of traditional quilts, it is
apparent that their unknown makers were masters of
composition, pattern, repetition, and color. Studying
the forms of the Victorian crazy quilt, one can recognize a long history of experimentation.

Great art quilts explore these ideas, expanding
the concepts and making us think about them in new
ways, sometimes ironically. They ask us to consider the
role of women's traditional arts. They present color
and material, play with pattern or revel in structure
and texture, but with emphasis on and attention to the
history from which they arose. The artists presented
here are in full control of their medium. Their works
demand the rightful place of quilts as an art form.

1. Patricia Mainardi. *Quilts, the Great American Art.* (San Pedro:
Miles & Weir, 1978)

2. Susan E. Bernick. "A Quilt Is an Art Object when It Stands
Up like a Man." Cheryl B. Torsney, Judy Elsley, eds. *Quilt Culture:
Tracing the Pattern.* (Columbia: University of Missouri, 1994)

3. Penny McMorris and Michael Kile. *The Art Quilt.* (San
Francisco: Quilt Digest Press, 1996); Patricia Malarcher in
Surface Design Journal, and others.

4. Elaine Showalter. "Piecing and Writing," *The Poetics of Gender.*
Nancy K. Miller, ed. (New York: Columbia University Press, 1986)

Pauline Verbeek-Cowart

Just before traveling to Athens, Ohio, to judge Quilt National 2011, I familiarized myself again with the expressed intent of the show and the stated rules and guidelines for entry:

To promote the contemporary quilt by serving as a showcase for new work that provides the viewer with an appreciation of the variety of techniques and innovative trends in the medium of layered and stitched fabric. The jurors will select works that represent unique approaches to the medium and demonstrate the breadth and diversity of contemporary expressions. Visitors to Quilt National 2011 will see that the time-honored traditions are thriving and are being expressed in new forms as today's artists rise to meet the challenges of new techniques and materials.

Our mission was clearly stated: to select works that paid homage to the quilting tradition while embracing new forms of expression through innovative uses of new techniques and materials. I was excited by the prospect of seeing work that might inspire a new direction in my own work, or provide stimulation for my students. As a weaver I am interested in the possibilities offered through advances in technology as well as the structural or functional potential of new materials. New tools allow us to do things that were not possible before. What I am able to do on my jacquard loom would be unimaginable on a dobby loom. It is not so much the idea that new tools are better, because often they are not, but they entice us to ask questions and stimulate us to think of new ways to create and express our interests. I viewed the more than 1,000 entries with this mindset the first time around and I was initially disappointed. Not a single entry in my opinion represented that leap into new territory, or challenged conventional notions of the medium and stood as a radical new approach. Current dialogue in weaving and constructed textiles revolves around new (truly new, not just non-traditional) materials and the use of technology. Though I was not

expecting groundbreaking new approaches, I was hoping for some sort of embrace of these new materials and tools. I was prepared to see digital embroidery, laser cutting, conductive thread and light-emitting diodes (quilts are layered; there are pockets, perfect for hiding and holding wires and batteries), or photochromic pigments. These are just a few of the materials and processes that fiber artists are exploring at the moment (and have been for years).

Looking at all of the entries the second time around, I decided to put all of my preconceived expectations aside and respond to the similarities and differences in the work in front of me. The sheer number of entries in and of itself was a powerful indicator that time-honored traditions are indeed thriving. I was definitely impressed by the dedication and commitment of all of the artists who entered; there was a lot of work, and all of it new work, never shown in exhibitions or published before. A quilt is not something you conceive of and complete in a few days. The investment in time in most of the entries was mind-boggling. The quilts that have made it into the final selection all stand as works of art that deserve merit and praise as being the best examples of the breadth of possibilities currently being explored in the medium of quilting—a medium that does have its own vocabulary and judging criteria. Good compositional choices are essential, but the beauty of a delicately or intricately worked surface, the sensitivity to the selection or creation of fabrics and color, the inventive or playful use of pattern, and the power of scale all seemed to command equal attention.

As a final note to those whose work did not get selected this year, it is important to consider that most work in fiber does not translate well, nor is fully represented, in digital form, which is now the standard format for all competitions. The tactile quality in quilts is important and is often difficult to capture in the digital conversion. This gives unfair advantage to the quilts that are predominately photographic and representational. Full views of the entries can only be

Pauline Verbeek-Cowart

Silk Roots
2005

Sized Indian silk, cotton; hand woven jacquard

88" H x 27" W

Process and materials define my work. I weave because I am attracted to the process. Weaving engages both sides of my brain and technological advances constantly redefine what is possible in this medium. I create a physical object rather than a simulation on a surface. The color choices I make are informed by the feeling of the subject matter I am depicting. I am using photography in conjunction with weaving and this often prompts me to keep the work in black and white, or black and off-white. There is a certain drama and power in restricting colors to black and white.

judged on composition and color. If stitching, piecing, texture, or a special surface treatment are crucial elements in a quilt, they have to be visible in the detail shot. Many entries did not include a close-up that revealed this much-needed information, leading to the assumption that nothing else was there. Another consistent element in many entries was the uneven quality in work from the same entrant. What we see in our mind's eye is often more magnificent than what materializes in front of us, but occasionally a clear and finished thought manifests itself and we know it when the work is completed. It is okay to only submit one entry even if three are allowed. Submit your very best work and do not dilute your submission with work that is not resolved.

There is something to be said about a well-organized and seasoned organization like The Dairy Barn Arts Center and its showcase exhibition, Quilt National 2011. Logistics are figured out, support is in place, and the shared passion of so many people keeps a good thing going. It was an honor to have been invited as juror and as such become part of its long history.

Jurors' Bios

Eleanor McCain is a practicing internal medicine physician in Fort Walton Beach, Florida. Although her career has been in science, she has always sought a creative outlet, focusing on the art quilt after 1994. She has been an exhibiter in Quilt National five times. Ms. McCain's works can be seen in many public and private collections, including the Mint Museum in Charlotte, North Carolina. She lectures frequently on the art quilt, and has been featured in numerous publications, such as *American Craft, American Style, Shuttle Spindle & Dyepot, Southern Living, American Quilter,* and *Diversion* magazines as well as *Fiberarts Design Books Six* and *Seven*.

A class on composition at the Anchorage Museum of History and Art, taken in 1995, inspired **Nelda Warkentin** to become an artist. While working in the field of community development for the state of Alaska, she enrolled in art classes at the University of Alaska and attended workshops around the United States. After experimenting with various paints and techniques, she chose the art quilt as her medium. Many galleries, museums, and other venues, including the U.S. embassies in Moscow and Cape Town, South Africa, have exhibited her work. One quilt is currently on display at the U.S. NATO Embassy in Brussels, Belgium. Her quilts have been juried into Quilt National six times and in Visions, a California art quilt exhibition, six times. Two of her quilts received the Award of Distinction at Quilt Nihon in Japan. Another received the Domini McCarthy Award at Quilt National 2003.

Ms. Warkentin, whose quilts are in numerous public, private, and corporate collections, is treasurer of the Studio Art Quilt Associates, an international professional organization advancing the art quilt medium. Her gallery representation is in Anchorage, Alaska.

A native of the Netherlands, **Pauline Verbeek-Cowart** received her BFA (1982) in Fine Art from the Maryland Institute College of Art and her MFA in textile design from the University of Kansas (1995). After teaching at the University of Kansas, she joined the faculty of the Kansas City Art Institute, where she has been developing the area of constructed textiles since 1997. In 2008, she was appointed chair of the Fiber Department. Pauline served on the board of the Surface Design Association and coordinated two textile conferences (2000 and 2003), which took place on the campus of the Kansas City Art Institute.

Ms. Verbeek-Cowart is one of the leaders in the use of new technologies in hand weaving and is actively researching jacquard applications using industrial looms in the Netherlands and the U.S. Her academic and fine-art careers have garnered her numerous awards, including the Kansas City Art Institute's Excellence in Teaching Award (2007) and most recently the Kansas Arts Commission Master Fellowship in Visual Art/Fine Craft (2008). Her industrially woven work crosses boundaries between fine art and applied textiles and is directed toward structurally textured fabrics for apparel as well as home furnishings. She is cofounder of Studio Structure, a design house specializing in high-end artisanal fabrics. Ms. Verbeek-Cowart's work has been exhibited extensively in both national and international venues, including France, Germany, Japan, and Korea. Her work is in private, corporate, and museum collections, including the Smithsonian's Cooper Hewitt, National Design Museum. She has been featured in books and publications such as *Fiberarts Design Book, American Craft, Fiberarts, Surface Design Journal, Shuttle Spindle & Dyepot,* and *Textile Forum* magazines.

The Quilts

Barbara W. Watler

Hollywood, Florida

Banana Bloom
2010

Cotton/polyester blend, #5 perle cotton thread, whole cloth; hand stitched

52" H x 42" W

A class with Dorothy Caldwell renewed my interest in hand stitching. I like the juxtaposition between completely covering fabric with machine stitching and making hand-done, random running stitches into designs. My husband loved these little Lady Finger bananas and grew them in our back-yard for years. The exotic look of banana blooms intrigued me and I photographed them repeatedly. This quilt honors his love and support for my love of making art.

Kate Themel

Cheshire, Connecticut

Dandelion
2010

Cotton, acrylic tulle, rayon thread, dye; raw edge machine appliquéd, machine quilted

46" H x 33" W

This tiny plant is a marvel in adaptability and survival. We may complain about the pesky dandelions taking over our grassy lawns, but who can resist the temptation to make a wish and blow their fuzzy seeds into the air…knowing that they'll thrive wherever they land?

Britt Friedman

Oberlin, Ohio

Riverdreams
2010

Cotton, original photographs; digitally manipulated, ink-jet
printed, painted, machine quilted

30" H x 42" W

I have gradually become more interested in stretching
the fiber medium in new directions. My strong interest in
digital photography has provided a new vehicle of design and
expression. I would like my subject matter to be recognizable
but not literal, and I want it to express my viewpoint and
feelings while at the same time resonating with and providing
pleasure to the viewer.

Pat Pauly

Pittsford, New York

Pink Leaf 2
2010

Commercial and artist-made cotton; hand dyed, discharged, stamped, shibori dyed, direct dyed, monoprinted, machine pieced, machine quilted

77" H x 65" W

The printed surface juxtaposed to the painted surface, the line against the shape, the dark against the light—all these relationships make up the whole. I loved making this piece, and loved quilting it.

Carol Watkins

Boulder, Colorado

Reflections on Duality
2010

Cotton, tulle, acrylic paint, digital ground, original photos, pigment ink, rayon and polyester thread, cotton embroidery thread; digitally processed, inkjet printed, free motion stitched, appliquéd, program stitched

35" H x 76" W

Duality describes tension between two opposing forces. *Reflections* recognizes our willingness to observe and learn.

Whether drilling for oil, building communities in sensitive habitats, or polluting air and water, we are destroying that which makes life on Earth possible. This planet is amazingly beautiful, colorful, and able to nurture incredibly diverse life forms. The future depends on us. What will it be? Visually, the conflict is expressed through color contrast and tension between structure and flow.

Susan Brooks

Louisville, Colorado

Little Bird
2010

Cotton, thread, deconstructed silkscreen, soy wax resist;
machine pieced, machine quilted

51″ H x 31″ W

Little Bird was inspired by a poem with the same name,
written by my daughter, Chara DeWolf. Chara's love of
the written word has been stitched together with my love
of color and texture to express the story of a newfound
love. Does love liberate or imprison? Is our own "little bird"
trapped in the cage or soaring free?

Carol Goossens

New York, New York

The Conversation
2009

Silk, cotton, collaged sheer fabrics; machine quilted

25" H x 42" W

In the early morning light, a discussion ensues between two crows. Crows are known to be very social and family-oriented but one can only speculate what they are discussing over breakfast.

Wen Redmond

Strafford, New Hampshire

Leaping Point
2010

Pretreated digital cotton canvas, hand dyed perle cotton, photograph melded with painted canvas; digitally fused and printed, mounted with heavy stabilizer, hand tied book binding, sealed with UV medium and paint

32" H x 51" W

I am a process person. My process is fed by my love of being outdoors and photography. I can see the most exquisite scenes or combinations of patterns and want to share that beauty. My art represents these moments; they are what lies beneath. Each work is individual and a communication between my inner imagination and, later, the viewer. This communication is the dream, wish, and hope for my artwork.

Nancy Whittington

Chapel Hill, North Carolina

Leaf Arabesque
2010

Silk, dye, oil paintsticks, silkscreen dyes; resist dyed, painted and discharged, sketched

43" H x 69" W

For me, the surface is a place to connect the naturalistic with the symbolic. Typically I use one or two geometric shapes, plus the spaces in between them, to create "patterned narratives." Their stories are told not in words, but in the language of symmetry.

In this work, a familiar motif found in nature repeats itself in a pattern of growth. A simple change in symmetry (in the sixth vertical row from the left) yields an unexpected, vivid flowering.

Katherine K. Allen

Fort Lauderdale, Florida

<small>McCarthy Memorial Award</small>

Glass Garden (Diptych)
2010

Silk, buckram, ink, acrylic paint, screenprint inks; painted and stencil printed on whole cloth, hand stitched

54" H x 108" W

My art is a meditation on nature. From garden, wetlands, and woods, I gather the raw materials I use in creating my soft paintings. These imaginary botanicals and abstract landscapes are created by painting and printing in successive layers on un-stretched cotton canvas or silk. Marks made by hand, brush, and stitch interweave with natural forms from the earth to communicate time, memory, emotion, and my philosophy of coexistence in harmony with nature. My goal is to create an evocative artwork that nourishes mind, eye, and spirit in equal measure.

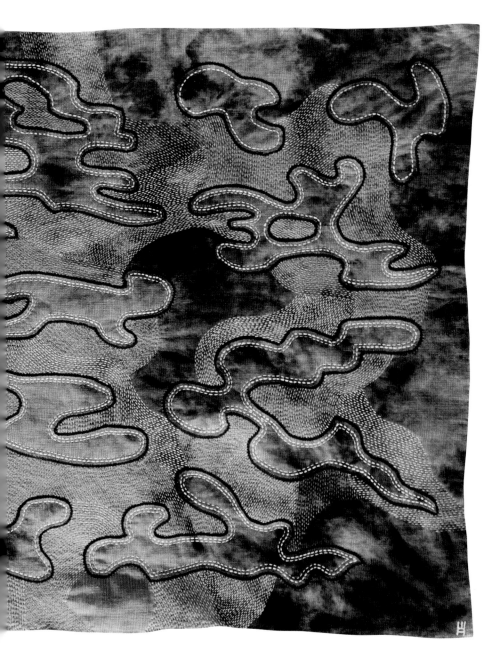

Anne Woringer

Paris, France

Ciel de Traine
2009

Vintage indigo cotton from China;
nui-shibori dyed and discharged

32" H x 64" W

This quilt is part of a series about the
sky. I love so much the indigo that I
use it as a metaphor for sky or water.
But I don't want to make a real sky, as
my work has always been abstract.

Kim Shearrow

Powell, Ohio

Sunrise at Age 45
2010

T-shirts, jacket, mesh fruit bags, chocolate wrappers, plastic bags, maxi-pad
wrappers, metallic thread; hand woven,
hand quilted

105" H x104" W

Sunrise is the symbol for new beginnings. At age 45, many things having ended,
I had a new beginning. This piece is made up of clothing that I felt society wanted
me to wear, fabric scraps from quilts made before I allowed myself the freedom to
not plan but just cut, plastic maxi-pad covers that I will never need again, fingernail
polish that I would never be caught dead wearing anymore, and chocolate wrappers
that got me through it all!

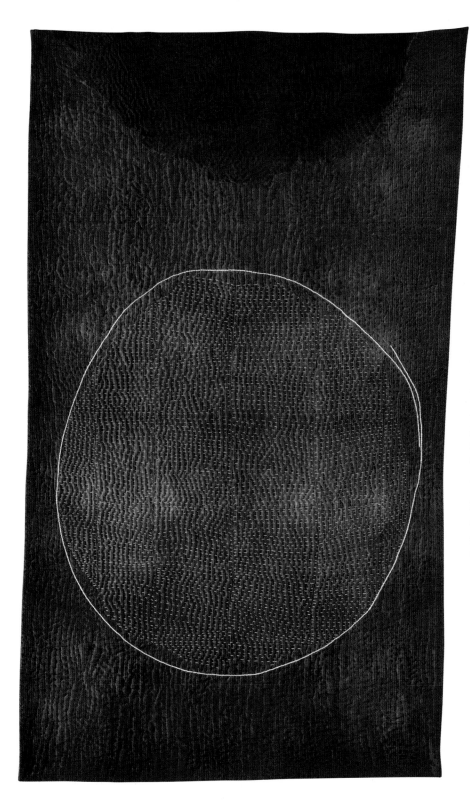

Pamela Fitzsimons

Mount Vincent, New South Wales, Australia

Werekata Moon
2010

Silk, silk thread; plant dyed, layered, machine
and hand stitched

43" H x 25" W

Nature's cycles continue in a parched continent. We must learn to tread more carefully on this fragile land before it is too late. The moon will still rise.

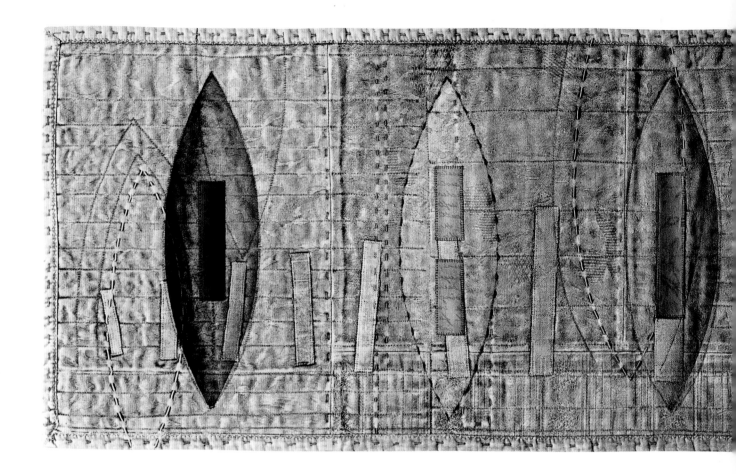

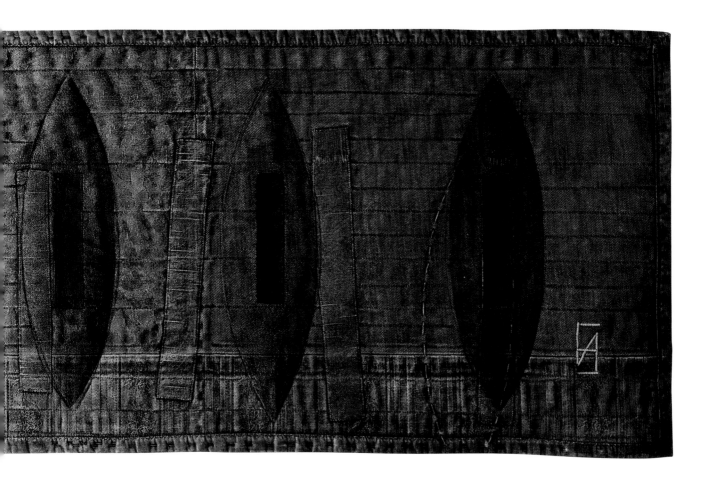

Heather Allen-Swarttouw

Asheville, North Carolina

Lunar Transition II
2010

Cotton, linen, dye, textile ink; collaged, dyed, painted, hand and machine silkscreened, hand and machine embroidered

13" H x 48" W

A boat symbolizes a journey and a vessel can symbolize self. The vessel is a metaphor of interior and exterior, of containment, of transport and journey, and as a tool—like the boat or tatting shuttle—has the ability to create. It is both universal and personal. The vessel and boats allow me a vehicle to investigate new ideas, narratives, and relationships.

Barbara Schneider

Woodstock, Illinois

Reflections, Variation 13, Honfleur, France
2010

Cotton, dye, thread, original photo-graph, fusible web, cotton batting; photo enlarged and interpreted, fused collage, machine stitched, drawn paint lines

58″ H x 42″ W

My *Reflections* series explores the concept of reflection and how to capture the essence of images that are not physically there, images made of light and movement, images that are infinitely variable. What does the eye see? What does the camera see? What does the mind see?

Marti Plager

Louisville, Kentucky

January
2010

PFD cotton, cotton batting, fiber-reactive dyes, flour paste resist; dye painted, machine quilted

39" H x 43" W

January is based on a photograph I took on a frozen lake in northern Minnesota. While hiking on the lake in snowshoes for the first time, I became fascinated by the pattern within the ice. One could think you were looking at a galaxy in space instead of 24 inches of frozen water. The patterns of the universe are repeated in so many different ways.

Paula Kovarik

Memphis, Tennessee

Global Warming, The Great Unraveling
2009

Recycled bed sheets, plastic grocery bags, baby blanket binding, cotton batting, cotton thread; whole cloth, hand and machine quilted, tea stained

51″ H x 40″ W

Shrinking polar ice caps, oil exploration in pristine wilderness areas, temperatures rising…when does it end?

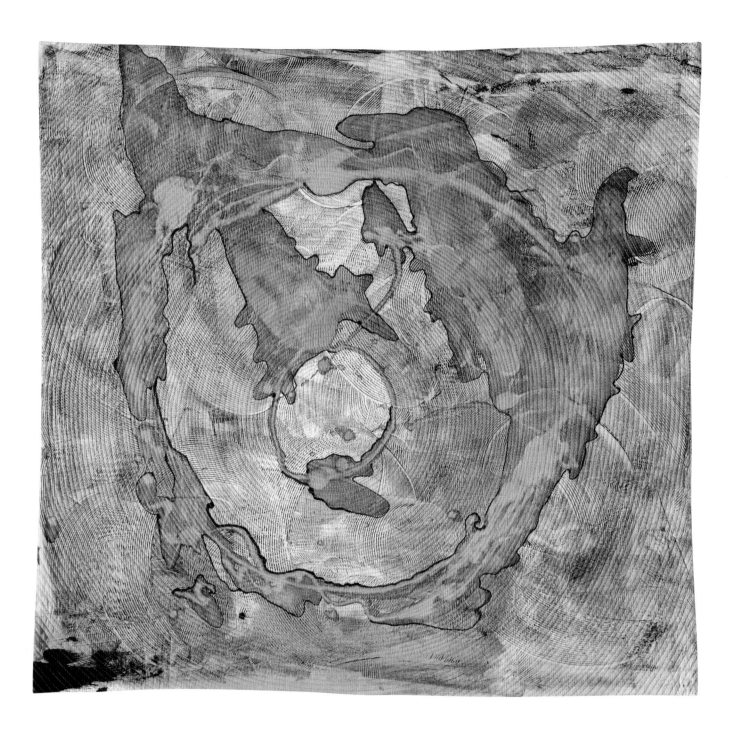

Caroline Szeremet

Hebron, Kentucky

Oil Spill
2008

Cotton, fiber-reactive dyes; whole cloth, monoprinted,
thickened-dye painted, machine quilted

33" H x 34" W

Oil Spill is a single-piece quilt produced by monoprinting and
painting fabric using fiber-reactive dyes. The process is both
challenging and exhilarating because the dyeing and curing
steps often produce surprising results. The title comes from
the impression this work naturally evokes.

Elin Noble

New Bedford, Massachusetts

JUROR'S AWARD OF MERIT

Fugitive Pieces II
2009

Cotton, silk, cotton thread, dye; itajime shibori (clamp resist); discharged, over-dyed, machine quilted with hand-dyed thread

78" H x 40" W

Fugitive Pieces II is a whole cloth quilt. It is itajime shibori, which for me involved layering patterns by repeatedly adding and subtracting colors, leaving hints and marks of what was there before. This method of dyeing allows me to juxtapose soft and hard edges, revealing an unexpected dance of solid and diffuse contours. Through machine quilting I accentuate color nuances, playing cloth and thread against one another. Overall, I aim for subtle narrative spaces.

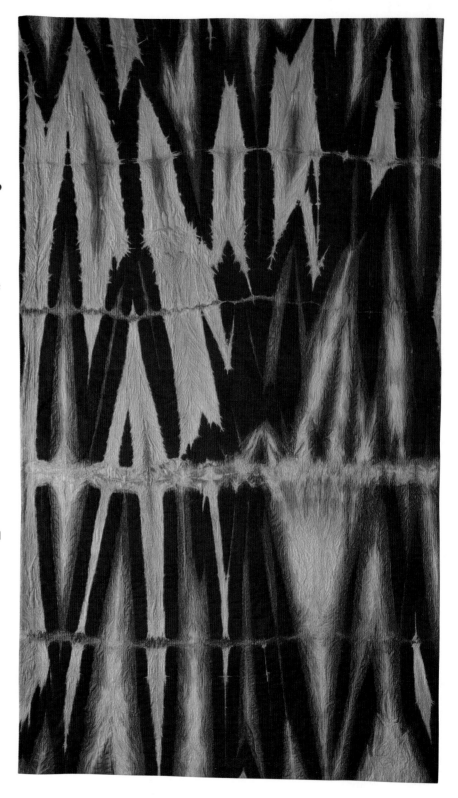

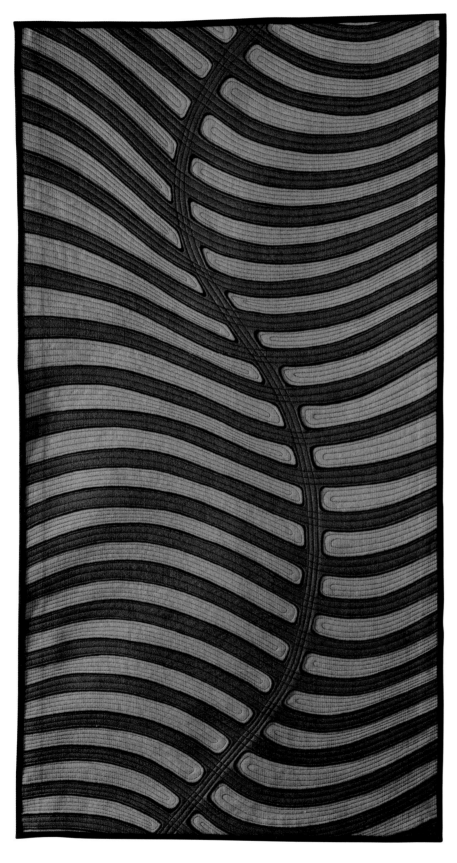

Dianne Firth

Canberra, Australian Capital Territory,
Australia

Earth Bones
2010

Wool felt, viscose felt, cotton, polyes-
ter/cotton thread; reverse appliquéd,
machine quilted

62" H x 34" W

Australia is a very old continent.
Mountain ranges that have been worn
down by the forces of nature capture
memories of an ancient past. This quilt
uses the metaphors of an animal and
plan (aerial) view to imagine the landscape as the remains of a giant, sleep-
ing beast.

Heide Stoll-Weber

Frankfurt/Main, Germany

King Lake 3: Ghost Trees
2010

Cotton sateen, silk organza, wool/
rayon felt, dye; machine pieced,
machine quilted, hand appliquéd

74" H x 74" W

Black Saturday, February 7th of 2009, was the day of the most devastating bush
fires in Australia to that date. Particularly struck was the small town of King Lake,
about 70 kilometers northeast of Melbourne. Seven weeks later I shot an exten-
sive series of photographs of the completely destroyed bush, which looked like
black-and-white photos even though they were taken in color. The air still smelled
of cold ashes and the completely charred trunks of the gum trees resembled
sculptured statues.

Bonnie M. Bucknam

Vancouver, Washington

BEST OF SHOW

Crater
2010

Cotton, dye; machine pieced, machine quilted

60″ H x 81″ W

I find inspiration in the landscape of the many places where I have traveled and lived. Each location has its own unique character, colors, and mood.

Janet Bass

Pittsburgh, Pennsylvania

Nature's Rorschach
2010

Cotton, fiber-reactive dyes; shibori dyed, (under-painted then then arashi-dyed)

39" H x 97" W

Quilting was never something I expected to do. Dyeing fabric is what inspires me and keeps me going. However, the latest results seem to be driving me to do larger pieces and quilting seems the best way to display them. I continue to struggle with the quilting so it doesn't get in the way of the fabric, yet carries the feeling forward. I love that these patterns provoke different images, depending on the viewer's experiences, and that one can continue to discover something else of interest.

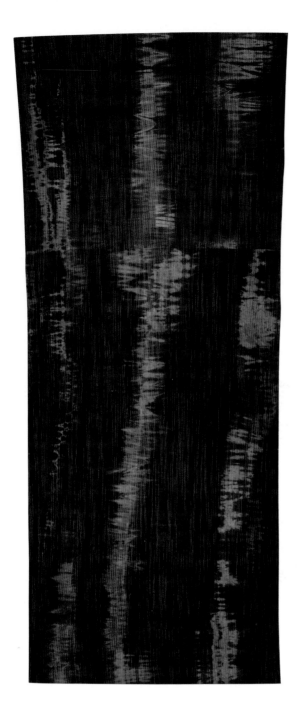

Helene Davis

Paducah, Kentucky

Shimmer 21
2010

Cotton broadcloth, dye, thread, batting; machine pieced, machine quilted

104″ H x 92″ W

Reflections, especially on water, point me to alternate realities and the reveries that feed my work begin.

Beth Carney

Yonkers, New York

Chasms 2: Fine Line 'Til Spring
2010

Cotton, dye; machine pieced, fused, machine quilted

37" H x 28" W

Chasms 2: Fine Line 'Til Spring is a piece made of contradictions, smooth thin lines that disappear and then reappear. These lines are set in color bars with ragged edges that remind us that there is a fine line between joy and sorrow as we say goodbye to the way things were and wait with hope for what the future will bring.

Fenella Davies

Bath, North Somerset, United Kingdom

Sunsplash
2010

Cotton, scrim, cardboard, non-woven translucent web;
collaged, appliquéd, hand stitched

47" H x 65" W

My pieces are designed to give a sense of place and
mood, but pared down to a simple design element: the
relationship of form and space. Implications of the past
are a recurring theme—traces of history and places—
to give a hint of what might have been, but ultimately
leaving the definition to the viewer.

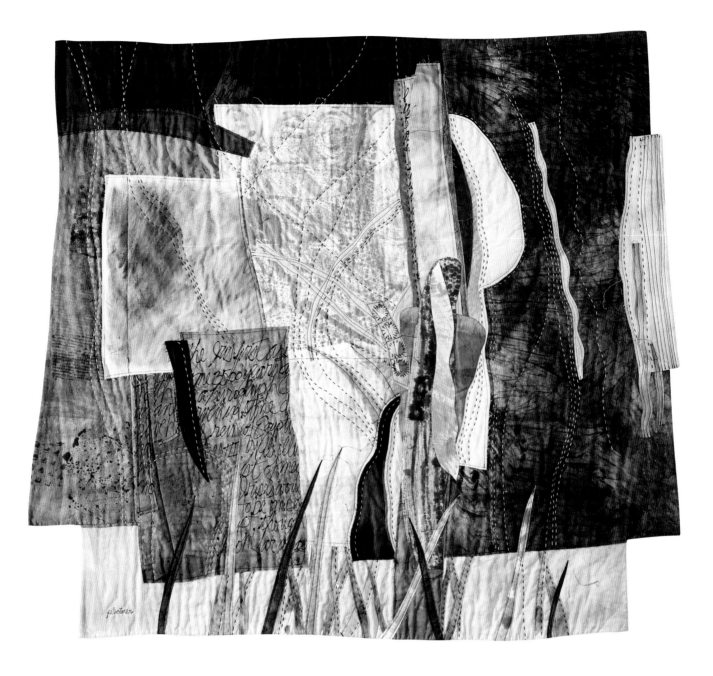

Judith Plotner

Gloversville, New York

Soul of an Iris I
2010

Cotton, polyester; hand-dyed, printed, painted, machine
pieced, appliquéd, machine and hand quilted

51″ H x 57″ W

Exploring a deeper vision of the world around me, my work
reflects my inner responses to my experiences. Expressing
what I feel is the soul of this flower, using color and form
to convey my feelings. I am trying to bring to the work a
personalized impression. I spend a lot of time in my garden
and am enthralled by the complicated shape and depth of
irises as yet another example of the life around us.

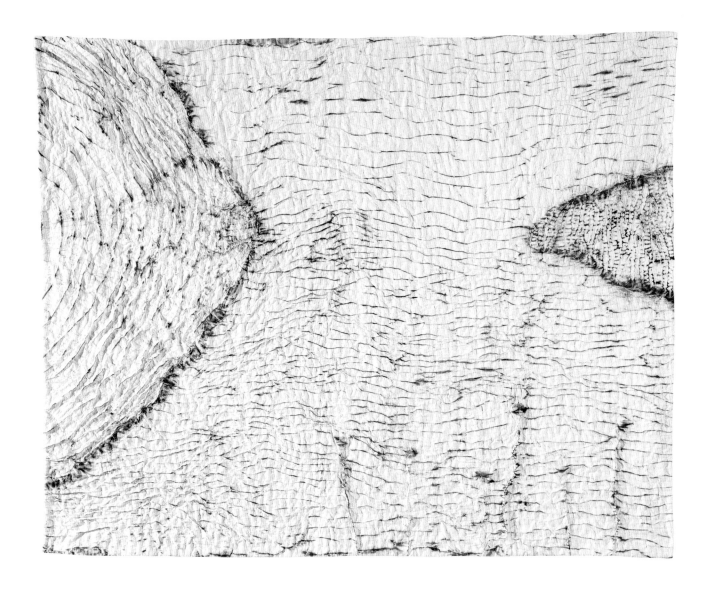

Sue Cavanaugh

Columbus, Ohio

Lynn Goodwin Borgman Award for Surface Design

Ori-Kume 20
2010

Organic cotton sateen, 4-ply spun silk, beading cord, fiber-
reactive dye, cotton batting, cotton backing; whole cloth,
shibori stitch resisted (ori nui and a variation of mokume),
dye painting, shibori stitch texturing, layered, hand quilted

41" H x 52" W

Life ebbs and flows, much like a river. We're ever changing,
yet, once a path is chosen, we tend to stay within the
comfort of our boundaries. Bits of the environment rub off
on us and enrich our journeys. And once in a great while
we might escape our imaginary banks and forge a new path.
Those times can make all the difference.

Dominie Nash

Bethesda, Maryland

Big Leaf 24
2010

Cotton, silk organza, textile paint, leaf rubbings; machine appliquéd, machine quilted

74" H x 69" W

I am fascinated with the shape, structure, and variety of leaves. I found some very large leaves that led to a new series. The leaves take center stage, enhanced by accidental patterns created by printing tools, variable amounts of paint, etc.... The relationships between the leaves comprise an important element of the composition. Friends and family bring me leaves they find, adding an element of collaboration. I enjoy the spontaneity of working with whatever comes along.

Louise Silk

Pittsburgh, Pennsylvania

Tree of Life
2010

Knit t-shirt remnants, perle cotton; machine pieced,
hand quilted

64" H x 78" W

This is a visual representation of the Tree of Life from the Jewish mystical tradition of kabbalah. The tree describes the primordial energy through which all things are created. Five values of color embody each of the levels or worlds. These are repeated in sections to symbolize the ten divine attributes. Knit t-shirt scraps, which under normal conditions are very difficult to work with, came together effortlessly to fashion a freeform tree.

Rosemary Hoffenberg

Wrentham, Massachusetts

Mt. Desert Isle
2010

Cotton; shibori dyed, over-dyed commercial fabric, marbled, screen printed, machine pieced, hand and machine quilted

53" H x 38" W

I begin by manipulating fabric into an arrangement that I can work with. There is an interplay of color and form that develops the piece into a cohesive statement.

Deidre Adams

Littleton, Colorado

Façade VII
2010

Cotton, acrylic paint; machine quilted, hand painted
40" H x 67" W

I explore ideas of time and transformation, inspired by the structural elements and seductive surfaces of old buildings and walls. An old wall tells a story, like a canvas upon which both nature and human beings play and leave their marks. Over the course of many years, layers of paint and graffiti are applied, only to be eroded by sun, rain, and wind. The result is a surface rich with texture and color.

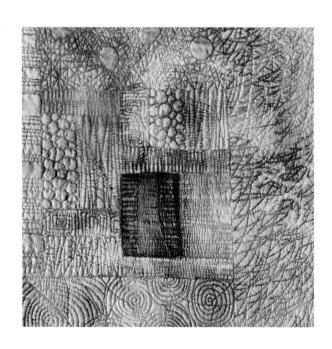

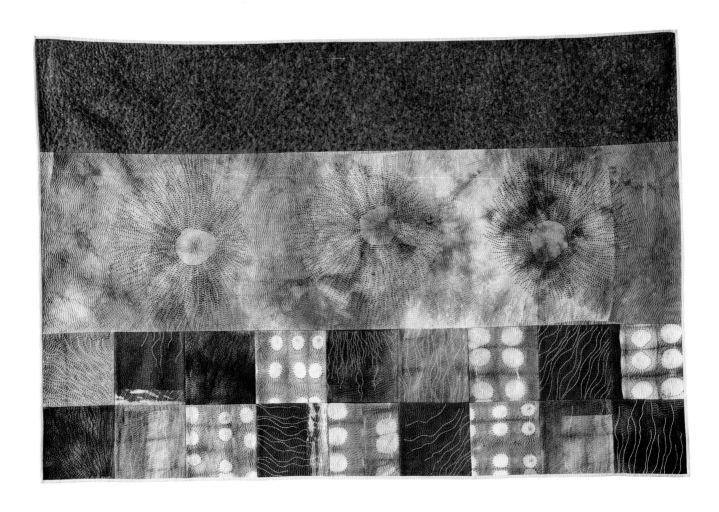

Carolyn Sullivan

Bundanoon, New South Wales, Australia

Mushroom
2010

Wool, silk, cotton; plant dyed, shibori dyed, hand stitched

37" H x 55" W

Mushroom represents the wide vistas of the land, the variations within the endless sameness of the Australian Bush, the tiny things that grow and live in my own small place, and the colors that the plants release into cloth.

Glenys Mann

Tamworth, New South Wales, Australia

Memory Cloth #11: Worn
2010

Wool blankets; plant dyed, hand stitched
75" H x 75" W

Worn: impaired by wear, use or exposure; showing the results of attrition. Ingrained by attrition or exposure to weather. (Source: *Shorter Oxford Dictionary:* 1933.)

Alison Muir

Cremorne, New South Wales, Australia

Ancient Messages
2010

Recycled silk kimono linings, polyester wadding, hand-dyed silk thread, eucalyptus-dyed cloth; hand painted, hand stitched (kantha stitch)

39" H x 37" W

Textiles impart subliminal messages, some of which emanate from when the cloth was used to protect the skin. Cultural messages have a similar longevity.

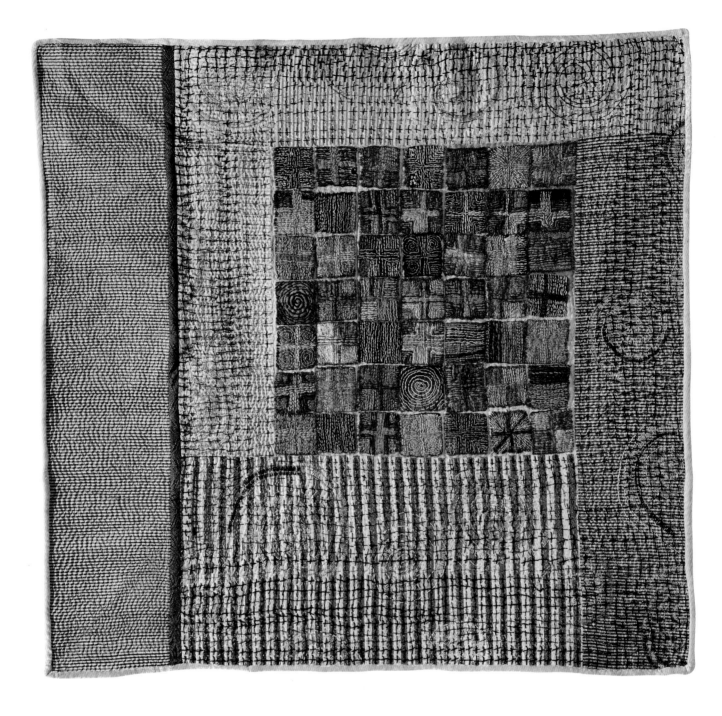

Judy Martin

Sheguiandah, Ontario, Canada

Cross My Heart
2010

Silk, linen, velvet, silk thread, dye, paint; layered, pieced, hand embroidered, hand quilted

33" H x 35" W

Hand stitching adds the power of repeated human touch. The small marks are each unique yet all the same.

Covering a surface with hand stitches gives me time to meditate. The "work" of the work also seems to open up a contemplative place for the viewer.

Time is taken to make the work.

Time is needed to understand it.

The time that I put into the work is a gift.

Time is a material.

Kevan Lunney

East Brunswick, New Jersey

Archeology: Fragment #14, Enso
2010

Linen, cotton and rayon thread, bamboo batting, paint, metal leaf; stenciled, hand quilted, frayed, shrunk, painted, leafed

54" H x 48" W

In 1896, 50,000 papyrus documents were discovered buried in mounds in Oxyrhynchus, Egypt: 1,000 years of daily records, inventories, news, and even jokes. They are now at Oxford University.

Enso is inspired by the idea that our own documents may someday be uncovered. Although the artifact is not decipherable, the aged gold patina optimistically infers value and wisdom. Imagine living in the year 4010, and upon viewing it, contemplating messages from the past. What meaning would you glean?

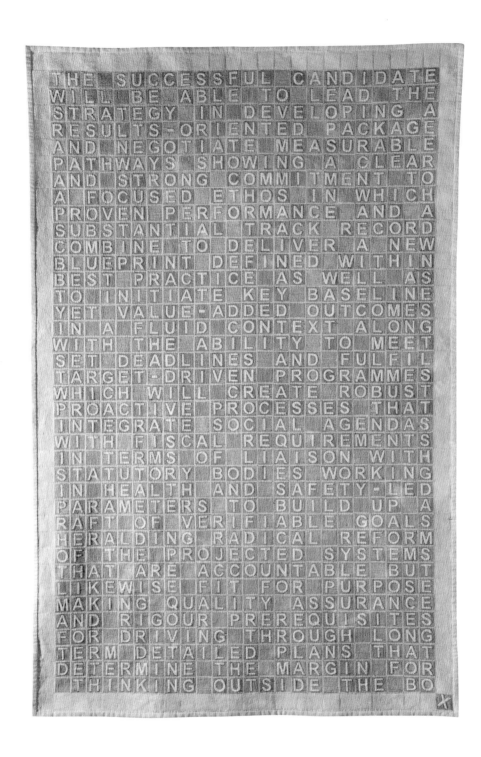

Sara Impey

Colchester, Essex, United Kingdom

Tickbox Culture
2009

Cotton; whole cloth, hand dyed, machine quilted

80″ H x 53″ W

This quilt is a response to today's so-called "tickbox culture," whereby pre-set targets and requirements, which must be achieved at all costs, supersede qualities like imagination, initiative, common sense, and experience—sometimes to the detriment of the service being provided. I wrote the text in the form of an advertisement for a meaningless job, trying to incorporate as many examples of "management-speak" as possible.

Daphne Taylor

New York, New York

Juror's Award of Merit

Quilt Drawing #13 – for Maureen
2010

Silk, cotton, polyester batting, cotton thread; whole cloth, hand quilted, hand embroidered

47" H x 39" W

In my *Quilt Drawing* series I honor my love of drawing. Lines reminiscent of landscape are quilted and embroidered with open white spaces. The rich visual language of these lines and markings is influenced and restrained by the power of simplicity. Hand quilting is of great importance in my work because it is equivalent to the act of drawing. The quilting is a loose, spontaneous act. My hand responds to the cloth, creating a loose rhythm of shadow line that is simple, clear, and meditative.

Linda Levin

Wayland, Massachusetts

In my work I try to capture a moment in time and a sense of place.

City With Footnotes XII
2010

Cottons, blends, textile paint; painted,
stitched with raw edges exposed

34″ H x 42″ W

Sue Cunningham

Stawell, Victoria, Australia

ReMarks 1
2010

Silk dupioni, silk organza, manipulated digital images;
printed, machine embroidered, machine pieced,
machine quilted

45" H x 52" W

This quilt is based on digital images of graffiti from Sisters
Rocks, near Stawell. It documents the passage of time. There
is the evidence of human presence, with layers of text and
marks slowly accumulating to create an evolving patina.
These defiant personal legacies feature generations of mark
making which overlap and embellish. The constantly changing
self-expressions are on the brazen, wild side and are perhaps
a rite of passage for some.

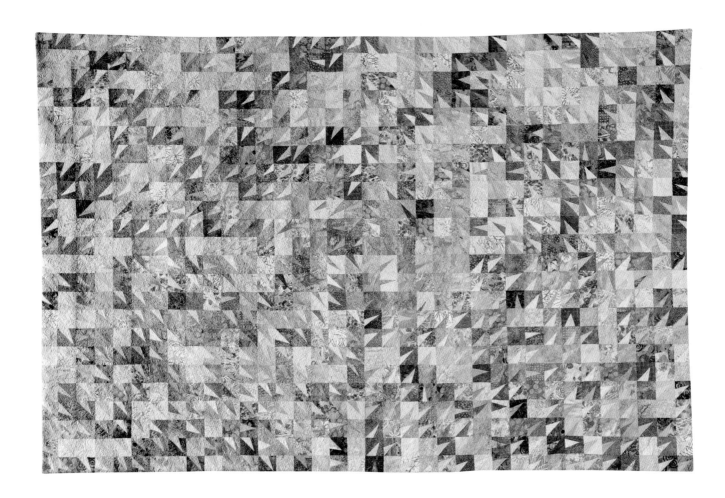

Mary Beth Frezon

Brainard, New York

Solveig
2010

Cotton, silk; machine pieced, machine quilted

46" H x 70" W

I feel the flush of my old love
The fabric squares in my hand
The rush as yellow returns
The slam of blue.

Benedicte Caneill

Larchmont, New York

Units 20: City Lights
2010

Cotton, textile paint, wool batting, cotton and polyester threads; monoprinted with a plexiglas plate, textile paints, and texture tools, machine pieced, machine quilted

54″ H x 54″ W

The *Units* series explores the construction of a whole piece using elemental geometric units which, when joined, establish the structure for lines and colors to interact. Fabric designs are monoprinted then cut and sewn back together using a traditional grid. The final composition develops in the process, with each piece unique, some more organic, others more architectural. *Units 20: City Lights* reflects my vision of urban architecture, with its ever-changing patterns of light.

Ann Rebele

Columbus, Ohio

Forgotten But Not Gone: Mary Ester
2010

Silk organza, fabric ink pens, hand-printed and hand-dyed
cotton, digitally enhanced original photograph, artist
pen-and-ink drawing, cotton and invisible thread; printed,
machine pieced, machine quilted

46" H x 36" W

While visiting New Orleans, I toured the area devastated
by Hurricane Katrina and made a visit to St. Louis Cemetery
No. 1, in the French Quarter. I was captivated by the texture
of the aboveground tombs, with their crumbling plaster surfaces and exposed bricks. Most had lost their "name plaques."
I thought about all of those buried there, all of the victims of
Katrina and other world disasters, and wondered if anyone
remembers who they were.

Inge Mardal and Steen Hougs
Chantilly, France

La Tristesse Damals and Today
2010

Cotton, thread, fabric paint; whole cloth, painted by hand, machine quilted

48" H x 71" W

This quilt is a reflection on the endless sadness and losses of war. With its mirrored, World War I motif and its title composed of three languages (French, German, and English), meaning "Sadness Then and Today," we point to the fact that sufferings of war are attributed to all parties involved—and not only to the final loser of the war.

Tanya A. Brown
Sunnyvale, California

Farmer Brown
2010

Cotton, paint, ink, wool/polyester batting, thread, homemade
soymilk resist; painted with watercolor and ink, quilted

40" H x 50" W

The birth of an elusive grin, as seen on untidy little
boys everywhere.

There is joy in bringing a blank piece of cloth to life,
in capturing a moment out of time or a bit of a person's
personality. Paint and ink combine to create shading,
with texture imparted by the stitching of several miles
of thread.

Joan Sowada

Gillette, Wyoming

Full Measure

2010

Commercial cotton, hand painted cotton, batting, thread; fused, raw-edge appliquéd, machine quilted

27" H x 27" W

Is the world a safe place or is it not? Is there one girl or two? These are questions for the viewer to ponder. My intention is to show the female spirit, firmly planted and fully present.

Olga Norris

Basingstoke, Hampshire, United Kingdom

Ponder
2010

Cotton, cotton wadding, cotton thread; digital image drawn
and collaged, printed, hand quilted

35" H x 47" W

Body language is largely unconscious and often a revealing
indicator of innermost emotions and attitudes. Of course
as onlookers we must never forget that we can be mistaken
in our reading of the body language of others. Indeed,
our interpretation(s) can say more about ourselves and
our own story. I like to leave my work open to wide
individual responses, which one could well alter after
subsequent viewings.

Jayne Bentley Gaskins

Fernandina Beach, Florida

Solitude
2010

Cotton broadcloth, cotton and polyester thread, inkjet ink, felt, polyester fiberfill; thread painted, trapunto quilted, digital photo manipulation

24" H x 32" W

Solitude holds different meanings for each of us. Sometimes it's a hollow, lonely feeling, and other times a welcome respite. How do you see it today? Tomorrow? This piece doesn't shout a message, but rather opens a door for the viewer to personal thought, introspection, and imagination. Each viewer will come away with something different; there are no right or wrong interpretations.

Nancy Cordry

Federal Way, Washington

Crazy Dang Genes
2010

Cotton, dye; freehand cut with rotary cutter, machine pieced,
machine quilted

74" H x 76" W

While researching the BRCA1 gene, after the shock of finding
out that my daughter had been diagnosed with a gene muta-
tion, I came across several depictions of what gene structures
may look like. I was fascinated by the design of these structures and by the complicated sequencing of DNA. I found
myself making sketches and wondering how a gene protein
might be presented in my art. The sketches led to playing
with my fabric and eventually *Crazy Dang Genes* emerged.

B. Michele Maynard

Chapel Hill, North Carolina

Vera Loves Her Gun
2010

Cotton, silk, organza, found and recycled fabric; collaged with fabric shapes to construct imagery, drawn with machine embroidery

44″ H x 30″ W

Sometimes pieces won't resolve. They languish and then head to my "to be cut up" pile. *Vera* was one of those. Sitting there, too decorative, with no meaning. She was saved when my sewing machine motor burned out and I just painted. Last fall, I bought a new machine. Going through my pile of failures I found *Vera*, still waiting, but I knew what I wanted her to say. I finished the piece.

Carol Coohey

Coralville, Iowa

Embodied
2010

Cotton, batting, thread, fiber-reactive dye; hand painted, printed, drawn, machine pieced, machine quilted

39″ H x 67″ W

Embodied gives form to my spirit.

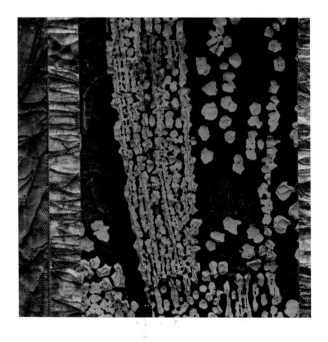

Judy Rush

Bexley, Ohio

QUILT SURFACE DESIGN SYMPOSIUM
AWARD OF EXCELLENCE

Portrait of the Youngest Girl 1
2010

Silk, cotton, and silk/rayon fabric,
woman's handkerchief, perle cotton, and
silk thread; stamped, screened, layered,
and cut

39" H x 25" W

After many years of learning how to
be a mother of children, I have yet to
figure out how to be a mother to my
adult children. This quilt is part of
a series that explores my children in
their adulthood.

Jean M. Evans

Medina, Ohio

JUROR'S AWARD OF MERIT

My Space
2010

Cotton, polyester batting, paint, embroidery thread; hand appliquéd, hand quilted, hand painted and embroidered

68" H x 46" W

As a fiber artist, I work with enthusiasm and patience, drawing from experiences and things imagined. Inspiration comes from within and from the observation of color, light, line, form, texture, and pattern on faces, figures, ordinary things, and nature. This quilt depicts "my imagined space" with chairs, dresser, fancy mirror, iron and ironing board, a window with curtains, a figure, and a table with a bouquet of flowers; it's full of color and abstract shapes.

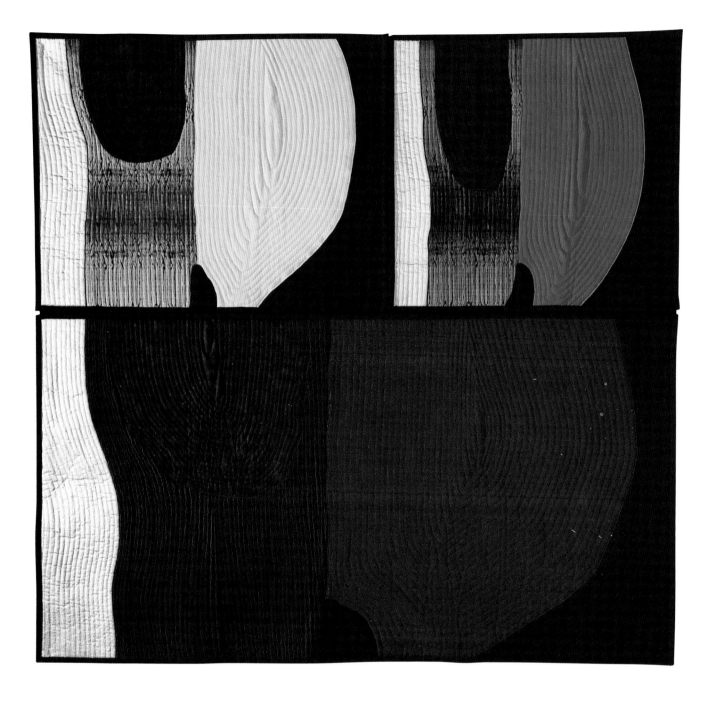

Bonnie J. Smith

San Jose, California

Color x 3
2010

Silk dupioni and cotton, polyester batting, polyester threads;
fused, machine appliquéd, machine stitched,
hand bound

48" H x 51" W

I create my designs with inspiration from nature. Once my designs are complete and I have achieved the right balance with the design, I move on to color. Laying out the color is the fun part—constantly working with fabrics, deciding which colors will bring excitement into the artwork, and trying to convey the gutsiest statement possible. I want the viewer to stop, take a look, and wonder. Wonder what? That part I leave to you, the observer.

Susan Shie

Wooster, Ohio

**Stars on the Water – The Oil Spill /
5 of Paring Knives in the Kitchen Tarot**
2010

Cotton whole cloth, fabric paint, thread, perle cotton
thread, bamboo-cotton batting, beads; painted, airbrushed,
paint brushed, air penned, fabric painted,
machine quilted

86" H x 79" W

I recorded events all through the first 100 days of the 2010
Gulf of Mexico oil spill, as well as other stories from that
period, in this piece. A mermaid sings a healing song, while
stars shine on the oily water, standing for hope and the Gulf's
beauty, before and after. The tarot card is about disaster and
a healing to come. Palm trees with strong paring-knife trunks
symbolize our future's clean energy windmills.

Marianne R. Williamson

Miami, Florida

Summer's Reflection
2010

Hand painted and commercial fabrics, batiks, thread
lace made with variegated thread and water-soluble
stabilizer; raw-edge appliquéd with monofilament zigzag,
thread painted

38" H x 38" W

My work is the reflection on water of light shining,
moving, dancing, and shimmering on a hot summer day.

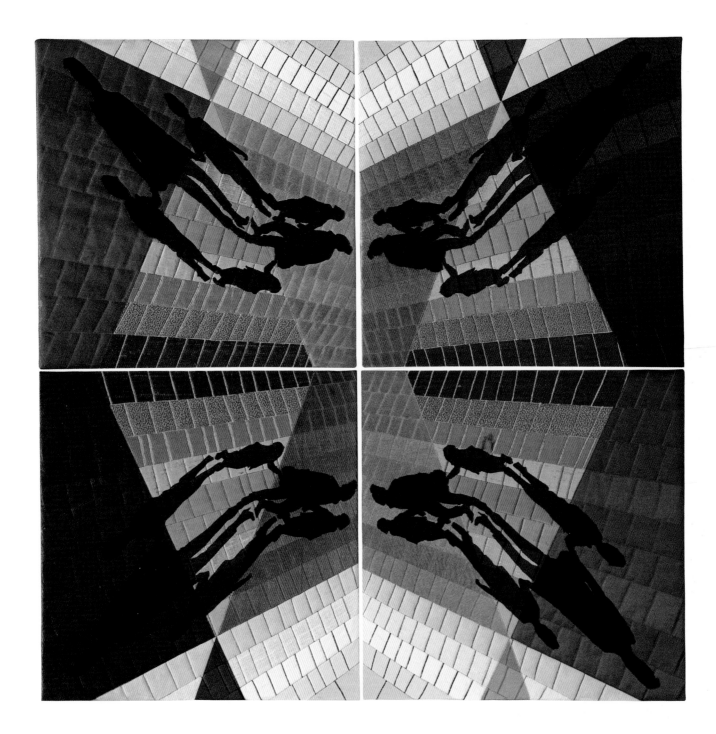

Cynthia D. Friedman

Merion, Pennsylvania

The Outing
2010

Silk, silk organza, fused organza; appliquéd, machine pieced, machine quilted, machined details

32" H x 32" W

I have always loved the geometry in block pattern quilts, especially in Amish quilts. I am also very interested in human body shapes and movement, and all those elements are part of my current series of *Shadowscapes*. I love working with the silks because of how they catch and reflect the light. The added focus on transparency, both literally and in terms of color, is my new obsession.

Lura Schwarz Smith

Coursegold, California

Granite Shadows
2010

Cotton, silk, cotton hand-dyed by Judy Robertson, cotton printed by Kerby Smith with designs by artist, perle cotton thread, digitally printed fabrics; machine pieced, machine and hand quilted

29" H x 36" W

I am intrigued by the way shadows echo and redefine form. A dry tree-branch shadow cast across granite stones by our river, in a black-and-white photo by my husband, Kerby, looked almost like a human figure. I enhanced the paper print with oil pastels to define the figure more clearly. Creating and digitally manipulating the colors of this image allowed me to convey a different reality.

Nancy Condon

Stillwater, Minnesota

Our Ladies of the Mountains
2010

Cotton/linen fabric, thread, digitally manipulated personal photos, digitally printed fabrics; stitched, machine assembled, machine quilted

35" H x 71" W

While traveling in Nepal down the Siddhartha Highway from Pokhara, in the Annapurna region, to Lumbini, the birthplace of Buddha, my driver, Yak, pulled over so I could use the latrine down the side of the mountain. As I climbed awkwardly down, I encountered these three women waiting for me to pass. I spoke no Nepali, they no English. Amid much smiling and laughter, I took their pictures and showed them. On the way back up, I got photos of them waiting for me to pass them again. I was enchanted by their intensity and joyful natures.

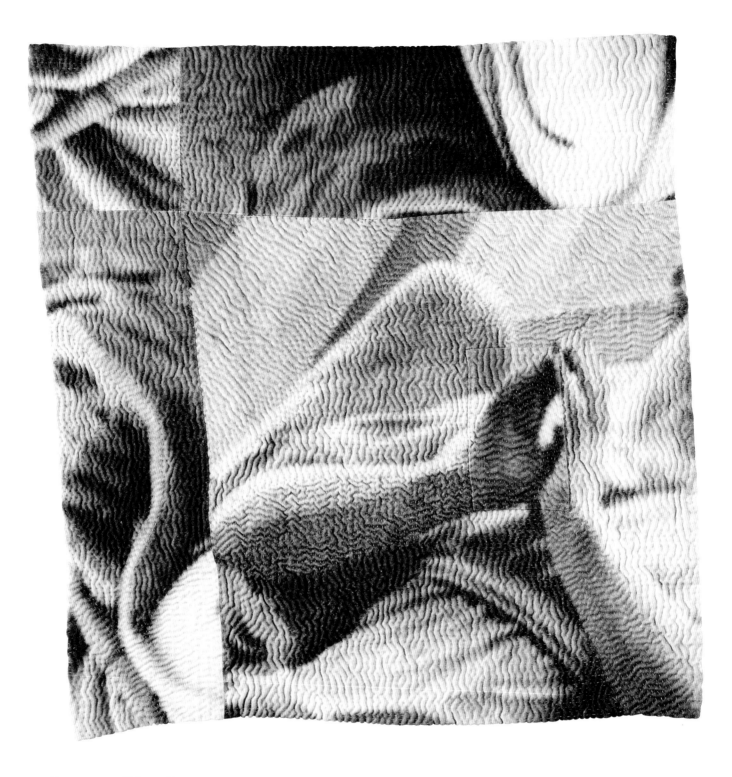

Luanne Rimel

St. Louis, Missouri

Venetian Stone 2
2010

Cotton flour sack dishtowel cloth, photograph, cotton batting; digitally printed, pieced, hand quilted, appliquéd

18″ H x 18″ W

Images of hands frozen in stone become metaphors for memory and existence. My photographs are printed onto prepared cotton with a wide-format inkjet printer. The image is divided and pieced, and detailed sections are created and layered, collaged and stitched onto the cloth, referencing earlier domestic practices of mending and repair, reuse and repurposing. The delicate, repetitive hand quilting across the surface creates shadows and textures and alludes to the marking of time.

Dinah Sargeant

Newhall, California

Fragments from the day gather in the night.

Pink Dog Blue Rain
2010

Cotton, cotton batting, ribbon, thread, fabric paint, resist; hand painted, direct
raw-edge and turned-edge appliquéd, embroidered, machine quilted

55" H x 57" W

Elizabeth Brimelow

Macclesfield, Cheshire, United Kingdom

Rook Road

2010

Silk, cotton; dyed, hand and machine stitched, appliquéd and reverse appliquéd, fused, screen printed, knotted, hand quilted

75" H x 36" W

At daybreak, hundreds of chattering rooks fly over my house traveling from their roosts to feeding grounds higher up the valley, returning at dusk. This quilt is a bird's-eye view of their daily journey. The format was inspired by John Ogilby, who in 1675 published the first road maps of England. Scrolled maps were designed to sit on the coachman's lap and be unwound as the journey progressed.

Alice Beasley

Oakland, California

Entre Nous
2010

Cotton, silk; raw edge appliquéd, machine embroidered, machine quilted

26″ H x 89″ W

In an era of twitting, tweeting, blogging, and Facebooking, are we losing the ability to communicate privately, one-on-one, simply *entre nous*? P.S. That's me on the end, on the right.

Judy Kirpich

Takoma Park, Maryland

CATHY RASMUSSEN EMERGING ARTIST MEMORIAL AWARD

Circles No. 4
2010

Cotton, dye, cotton and polyester thread; machine pieced, machine quilted

39" H x 35" W

Circles No. 4 explores the tension I have felt during the last two years of economic turmoil in our country. While my compositions may appear to be a random assortment of circles and lines, they are all placed quite deliberately. The technique I use involves cutting over and over into a "finished" top—my version of Russian roulette, since one false cut can, and has, ruined months of work.

Anne Smith

Golborne, Warrington, England

Mother me Mother you
2010

Recycled cotton, wool, thread, sequins, beads; hand pieced,
hand and machine appliquéd and embroidered, hand quilted

67″ H x 61″ W

Quilts are made over a longish time, during which Life casts
its influence on the work in hand. I made this quilt between
several 400-mile trips to visit my mum. I like to have an idea
in mind and improvise as I go along. The image began as a
baby elephant, but gradually she took on her own personality—that of an older and enduring lady. I even began to
think of her as "Betty."

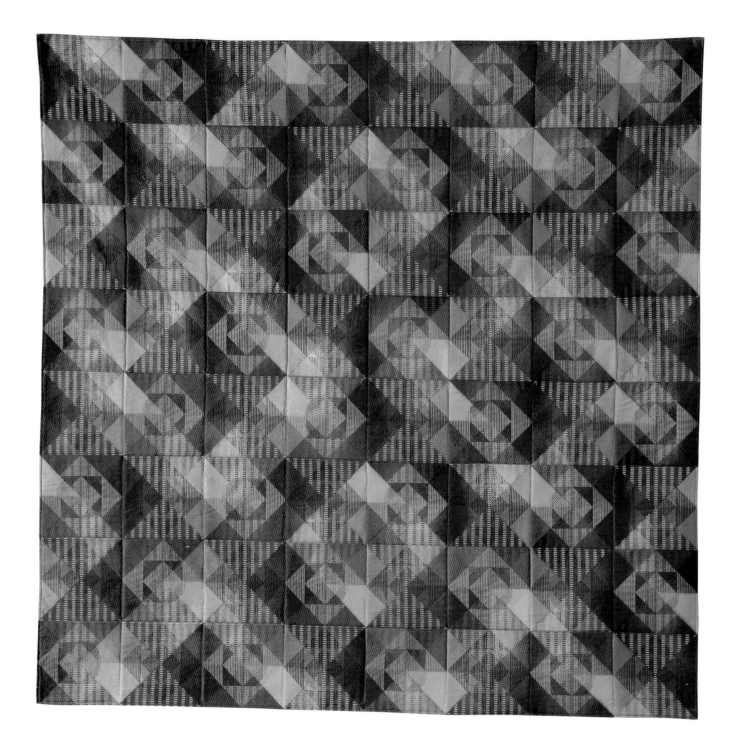

Ellen Oppenheimer

Oakland, California

BR #1
2010

Cotton, fiber-reactive dye, textile ink; screen printed,
machine pieced, machine quilted

62" H x 62" W

This quilt is a very simple idea—just a series of red and blue
squares and frames with an interlocking shadow of purple
squares and frames. I struggled with getting the color and
overlaying patterns the way I wanted for several years and
finally got close enough in the summer of 2010 to put the
quilt together. Here it is: still not exactly what I want but better than the first try, which is on the back.

Naomi S. Adams

Denton, Texas

<small>Most Innovative Use of the Medium</small>

Greek
2010

Cotton, dye, adhesives, batting, cotton thread; adhesive reconstruction, machine quilted

72" H x 54" W x 2" D

Greek speaks to my fascination with communication struggles in relationships. Our individual and shared experiences and influences affect how we understand and convey meaning. I am interested in exploring how constant change in our lives influences how we emotionally process emphasis, content, and context. I am intrigued with the process of creating, deconstructing, and then redefining a new composition from the parts of the whole to communicate the depth of our complex and evolving relationships.

Anke Kerstan

Berlin, Germany

Kaleidoscope II
2009

Cotton, blends, recycled checked and striped shirt fabrics; machine pieced, machine quilted

51" H x 71" W

I assembled kite-shaped pieces of the same material into hexagons. Depending on the chosen swatches of fabric, the hues and patterns of the hexagons change and, once combined in a patchwork, produce an effect similar to the one you get looking through a kaleidoscope: a crystal-like structure that is both balanced and dynamic.

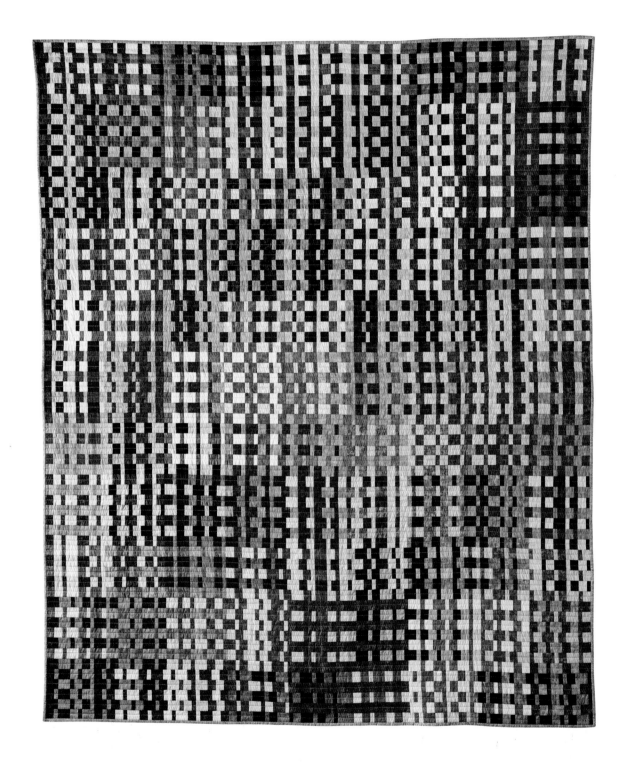

Kent Williams

Madison, Wisconsin

Checks Mix
2009

Cotton, cotton thread; machine pieced, machine quilted

82" H x 67" W

I've been playing with weaving textures, off and on, for several years. I like the suggestion of a weave that, upon closer inspection, is not there, only depicted. I know this puts me at odds with modernists who strove to boil art down to its essence—no lies!—but I seem to prefer illusion, trickery, deception. Oh, what a tangled web we weave....

Lisa Call

Denver, Colorado

AWARD OF EXCELLENCE

Structures #113
2008

Cotton, fiber-reactive dyes, cotton batting, cotton thread, hand dyed fabric; freehand cut with rotary cutter and/or scissors, machine pieced, machine quilted

39" H x 86" W

The *Structures* series, which investigates the boundaries we use to divide our world, originated as an exploration of human-made structures for containment, such as fences and stone walls. Lines of posts, negative space created between odd shaped stones, and uniform rows of bricks are all of interest.

As the series matures, focus has shifted to the psychological barriers humans use to protect themselves emotionally, exploring how we hide our true thoughts and feelings with these imagined roadblocks.

Bette Uscott-Woolsey

Philadelphia, Pennsylvania

52 Pickup
2010

Silk, thread, dyed silk; fused,
machine stitched

66" H x 43" W

Mix your colors. Prepare the surface.
Throw the colors on. See what happens.

Pat Budge

Garden Valley, Idaho

Compatibility
2010

Cotton, batting, thread; machine pieced, machine quilted

46″ H x 60″ W

Successful collaborators recognize that differences among individuals create outcomes greater than the sum of their parts. With *Compatibility*, the second in my *Anagrams* series, I found new synergy by combining various constructions in a new way.

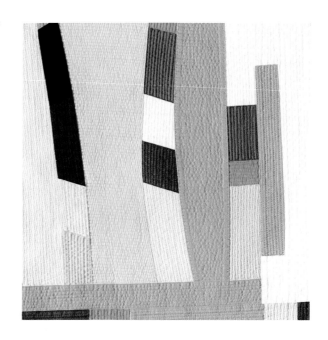

Shoko Hatano

Tokyo, Japan

PERSISTENCE PAYS AWARD

Color Box #13
2009

Silk, cotton, tulle, dye; painted, airbrushed, hand-dyed, machine
pieced, direct appliquéd by machine, machine quilted

54" H x 79" W

I have expanded my image of the transformation of the
social condition and environment with color, light, and
shadow. The joy of machine quilting also took part in
creating a scene of the mysterious and eternal cosmos.
I am concerned about the destruction of the natural
environment due to global warming.

Gay E. Lasher

Denver, Colorado

Abstraction II
2010

Paper-backed cotton sheeting, inks, poly/cotton thread,
digitally-manipulated photographic elements printed on
cotton; machine quilted

47" H x 31" W

As an artist I am concerned with ideas of transformation
and mystery, the boundaries between reality and illusion.
I am intrigued by the potential that even pedestrian images
or subjects have to be reborn in a new or different way.
My current work combines past experience, manipulating
photographic images with earlier work in textiles, and a
delight in the bas-relief nature of the quilted surface.

Katie Pasquini Masopust

Santa Fe, New Mexico

QUILTS JAPAN PRIZE

Con Brio – With Spirit
2010

Cotton, cotton blends, synthetic suede; machine appliquéd, machine pieced, machine quilted

64" H x 64" W

I have returned to my painting roots, working with acrylics while listening to music. These paintings are then translated into quilts that feature the original artwork as a centerpiece. The flow of my brushwork and the colors and patterns of my fabrics are the notes floating in the air.

Barbara Lange

Freising, Germany

Interlocked
2010

Cotton, dye, beads, copper wire, copper mesh; machine embroidered, machine and hand quilted, soldered, beaded

51" H x 32" W

In a quest to introduce new materials and techniques to my quilting, I came upon soldering as a method of connecting metal with fabric. It seemed to be the ideal combination to express my love for intense sewing on the one hand and technical science on the other. The pieced background is the detail of a maze—to me a symbol for time, just as the gear wheels are ticking away time.

Leslie Joan Riley

Skokie, Illinois

I focused on using color and pattern to create warm visual texture and a strong figure-ground relationship.

Broken Fence
2010

Cotton, dye, wool batting; machine pieced, machine quilted by Sue DiVarco, pattern designed by Leslie Joan Riley

72" H x 83" W

Patty Hawkins

Estes Park, Colorado

Lingering Image, Japan
2010

Cotton, cotton sateen, fabric paint, thermofax discharge paste; deconstructed screen printed, monoprinted, direct appliquéd with fusible web, machine quilted

44" H x 46" W

Walking on the pathway through 10,000 tall, wooden red *tori* gates in Kyoto (at the Fushimi Inari Shrine) truly overwhelms the senses. Because red has so many connotations, this vast red-orange structure is completely captivating and mesmerizing, especially when glints of sunlight peek through it. I honor my 2006 Quilts Japan Prize, which afforded this treasured memory as well as many lingering images. My deliciously nuanced fabrics add perspective.

Gail J. Baar

Buffalo Grove, Illinois

Lost and Found: Blue
2010

Cotton; hand dyed, machine pieced, machine quilted

39″ H x 45″ W

This is the first in a series of quilts focused on simplicity. We live in a world that is complicated and sometimes stressful. I strive to find what is simple and interesting. I have always loved squares. The meaning of the word *square*, whether used as a verb or noun, is interesting: to balance, harmonize, conform, or blend. This very agreeable shape, beautiful in its simplicity, helped me find what I was looking for.

Pat Oden

Sequim, Washington

9 Patch / 26 Triangles
2010

Cotton; machine pieced, machine quilted

47" H x 47" W

I love the simplicity of triangles and the versatility yet simplicity of the classic nine-patch form. Making this piece using big pieces or saturated color, rotating the patches until interesting, clear secondary patterns appeared, was fascinating. But then the playful side of me kicked in… counting all the triangles and trapezoids, squares and… just fun.

Jan Myers-Newbury

Pittsburgh, Pennsylvania

Firebox
2010

Cotton, cotton batting, fiber-reactive
dye; dyed in arashi shibori techniques,
machine pieced, machine quilted

46" H x 49" W

I'm fascinated by the spatial interplay of the shapes between transparencies created in the dye process and those created by piecing placement decisions. As has always been the case in my work, succulent color is the key ingredient. For me, the beauty of work is in the richness of detail as well as the message of the whole. I think I will never tire of exploring this simple technology: dye in a plastic bucket.

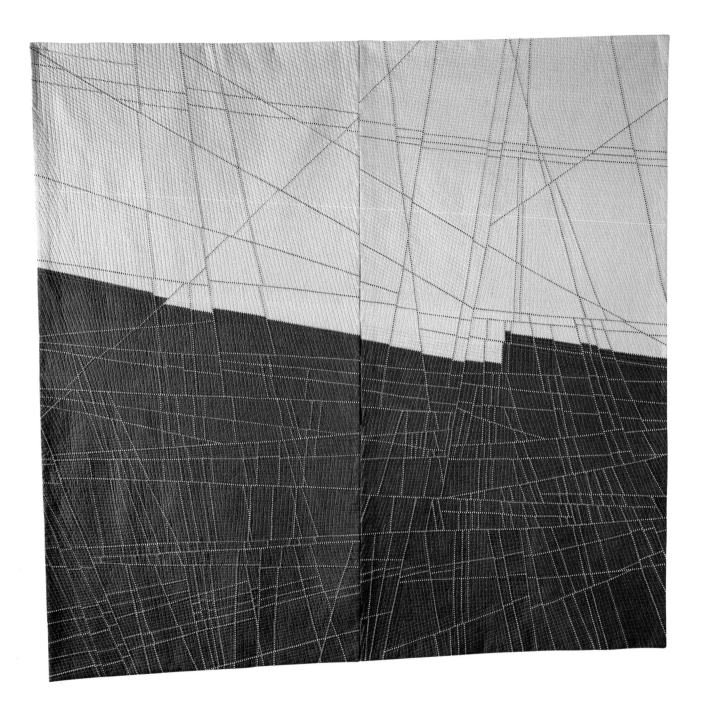

Kathleen Loomis

Louisville, Kentucky

Fault Lines 4
2010

Cotton, perle cotton; machine pieced, machine quilted,
diptych sewn by hand

76" H x 76" W

Much of our world is a mess these days, its economic, social,
and environmental stability threatened by disruptions,
stresses, slippages, and outright fractures. I hope it's not too
late to fix it, but we are so easily distracted by arguments
over who's to blame and who deserves to be rescued.

Mary E. Stoudt

Reinholds, Pennsylvania

THE HEARTLAND AWARD

Equilibrium
2010

Cotton, silk, velvet, unidentified fabric; raw edge
reverse appliquéd

55″ H x 35″ W

Since the 70s, I have been stitching, weaving, painting, and
exploring a wide variety of media. In 2003, I started layering
fabric in a grid-like fashion. I visualize the quilt composition,
its colors and forms in my head and then as I move through
the process, I improvise the details.

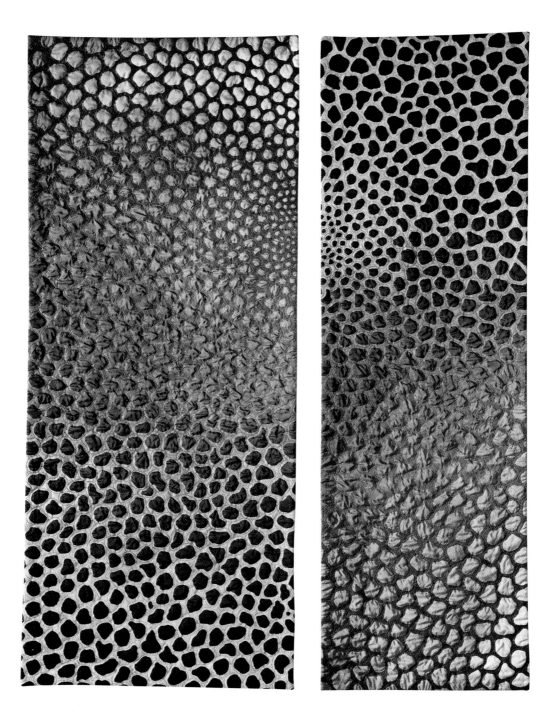

Betty Busby

Albuquerque, New Mexico

Opposites Attract
2010

Silk habotai, interfacing; acid dyed, hand painted, cut with
hot knife, fused

41″ H x 32″ W

I have long been fascinated by the unseen world of micro-
scopic images. *Opposites Attract* is an abstraction of such
images. I am attempting to produce a feeling of movement
and tension with the use of simple color gradients and subtle
alterations in pattern repetition.

About the Dairy Barn

Over nearly four decades, The Dairy Barn Arts Center has evolved into a first-class arts center with 6,000 square feet of exhibition space. Renovation architects retained the original character of the barn without sacrificing the design, climate control, or security features that make it a state-of-the-art, accessible cultural facility. In 1993 the Ann Howland Arts Education Center was built to house The Dairy Barn's growing art class and workshop program. A capital campaign led to the 2001 renovation and expansion of an additional 7,000 square feet, previously undeveloped, on the second floor. The space now includes five rooms for performing and visual arts classes and community events.

The Dairy Barn Arts Center's mission is to nurture and promote area artists and artisans, develop art appreciation among all ages, provide the community access to fine arts and crafts from outside the region, and draw attention and visitors to Southeast Ohio. The twelve-month program calendar includes international juried exhibitions, touring exhibits, festivals, programs of regional interest, live performances, and activities for all ages. Some events are produced entirely by The Dairy Barn Arts Center while others are the result of cooperation with regional education, arts, or community organizations. Exhibits such as OH+5 and Athens Voices feature outstanding, regionally produced artwork in a variety of media. The Dairy Barn Arts Center has also developed an international reputation for excellence with Quilt National, a biennial exhibition that has attracted more than 100,000 visitors to Athens from around the world since its premiere in 1979.

The Dairy Barn Arts Center is supported by admissions, memberships, corporate sponsorships, grants, and exhibition tours and art sales. The staff of seven is assisted by a corps of more than 200 volunteers, who donate thousands of hours annually.

The Dairy Barn Arts Center's top-notch exhibitions and programs, its reputation in the international arts community, its close proximity to Ohio University, and its picturesque setting make it an important stop on the itinerary of many visitors. The Dairy Barn Arts Center has added significantly to the Athens area's reputation as a cultural center. Both Athens and the Dairy Barn have been featured in the book, *The 100 Best Small Arts Towns in America*, and Athens was mentioned in USA Today as one of the ten best arts-centered communities in the country.

For a calendar of events and information about any Dairy Barn program, contact The Dairy Barn Arts Center, P.O. Box 747, Athens, Ohio, 45701; phone 740-592-4981; or visit the website at www.dairybarn.org.

Quilt Tour Itinerary

The complete Quilt National 2011 collection will be on display from May 23 to September 5, 2011, at The Dairy Barn Arts Center, located at 8000 Dairy Lane, Athens, Ohio. Three separate groups of Quilt National 2011 works (identified as Collections A, B, and C) will then begin a two-year tour to museums and galleries. Tentative dates and locations are listed below. It is recommended that you verify this information by contacting the specific host venue prior to visiting the site.

For an updated itinerary, including additional sites, or to receive information about hosting a Quilt National touring collection, contact The Dairy Barn Arts Center.

P.O. Box 747, Athens OH 45701
Phone: 740-592-4981
E-mail: artsinfo@dairybarn.org
Website: www.dairybarn.org/quilt

May 28, 2011 – September 5, 2011
Athens, Ohio; The Dairy Barn Arts Center

October 2, 2011 – November 4, 2011
St. Charles, Missouri; The Foundry Art Centre (A, B, and C)

February 14, 2012 – April 29, 2012
San Jose, California; The San Jose Museum of Quilts and Textiles (A and B)

Photo © Gary J. Kirksey

Index of Artists

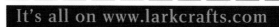